The month of January, from the Grimani Breviary

The Story of a Special Day
Volume 17

January

17

17th day of the year
348 days (349 in leap years)
remaining until the end of the year.

by Michael Dobson

Timespinner
Press

Table of Contents

Cover: The cover painting is "Benjamin Franklin Drawing Electricity from the Sky," by Benjamin Franklin. Franklin was born January 17, 1706—the EVENT OF THE DAY.

January 17 Quotations

"Whether it be dream or truth, to do well is what matters. If it be truth, for truth's sake. If not, then to gain friends for the time when we awaken."

— *Pedro Calderón de la Barca, dramatist and poet, born January 17, 1600*

"I wish the Bald Eagle had not been chosen as the representative of our country; he is a bird of bad moral character; like those among men who live by sharping and robbing, he is generally poor, and often very lousy. The turkey is a much more respectable bird."

— *Benjamin Franklin, polymath, born January 17, 1706*

"A man must have something to grumble about; and if he can't complain that his wife harries him to death with her perversity and ill-humour, he must complain that she wears him out with her kindness and gentleness."

— *Anne Brontë, novelist and poet, born January 17, 1820*

"A politician is a person with whose politics you don't agree; if you agree with him he's a statesman."

— *David Lloyd George, prime minister, born January 17, 1863*

"Fighting battles is like courting girls: those who make the most pretensions and are boldest usually win."

> — *Rutherford B. Hayes, 19th US President, died January 17, 1893*

"You can get much farther with a kind word and a gun than you can with a kind word alone."

> — *Al Capone, gangster, born January 17, 1899*

"God has given us our talents, not to copy the talents of others, but rather to use our brains and imagination in order to obtain the revelation of true beauty."

> — *Louis Comfort Tiffany, stained glass artist, died January 17, 1933*

"In a competition of love we'll all share in the victory, no matter who comes first."

> — *Muhammad Ali, boxer, born January 17, 1942*

"A lot of young people think they're invincible, but the truth is young people are knuckleheads."

> — *Michelle Obama, first lady, born January 17, 1964*

"The most difficult thing in the world is to know how to do a thing and to watch somebody else doing it wrong, without comment."

> — *T. H. White, author, died January 17, 1964*

Benjamin Franklin, by Joseph-Siffrein Duplessis (1778)

Event of the Day

Benjamin Franklin Born

The remarkable Benjamin Franklin was in a single lifetime a leading author, printer and publisher, political theorist, postmaster, scientist and inventor, statesman, and diplomat, as well as one of the Founding Fathers of the United States. A true polymath, or "Renaissance man," Franklin was not only notable for the range of his knowledge and talents, but also for his achievements. He has been referred to as "the most accomplished American of his age and the most influential in inventing the type of society America would become."

Benjamin Franklin was born on January 17, 1706 (O.S. January 6, 1705—see "On Names and Dates"), in Boston, Massachusetts. At age 12, he was apprenticed to his brother James, who founded the first truly independent newspaper in the colonies. At age 17, Benjamin ran away to Philadelphia to seek his own independence, working as a typesetter and printer. He founded a reading and study group known as the Junto, and when books proved too expensive for the membership, Franklin started one of the first libraries in the colonies.

In 1728, Franklin became publisher of the influential *Pennsylvania Gazette*, and later published books, including his own best-selling *Poor Richard's Almanack*, which featured much of his own writing and helped to cement his popularity. (John Paul Jones's ship *Bonhomme Richard* took its name from *Poor Richard's Almanack*.)

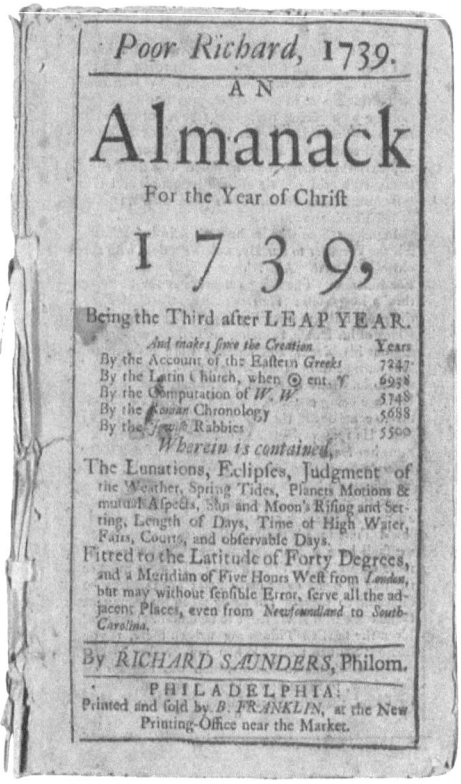

The 1739 edition of *Poor Richard's Almanack*

Benjamin Franklin was one of the leading scientists, inventors, and scholars of his era. He is perhaps best known for his proof that lightning is electricity, but while he described the kite experiment as a way to test his idea, there's no definitive evidence he actually flew the kite himself.

He was a prolific inventor whose creations included the lightning rod, the Franklin stove, and bifocal eyeglasses. He did pioneering work in demographics, oceanography, and meteorology. He developed anti-counterfeiting techniques for paper currency. He also wrote the first known description of a "pro-and-con" list. He played the violin, the harp, and the guitar, composed music, and built an improved glass harmonica. And he was the first chess player known by name in America.

In mid-life, Benjamin Franklin began moving away from his work as a printer and publisher, and became increasingly active in public affairs and politics. He founded one of America's first volunteer firefighting companies, established America's first hospital, and created one of the predecessors to the University of Pennsylvania.

The British government appointed Franklin as one of two Postmaster Generals of British North America. He made major management improvements and sped up service. Under Franklin, a colonial American could send a letter from Philadelphia to Boston in only a week! (Later, Franklin was the natural choice to become the first Postmaster-General of the newly formed United States of America.)

In 1757, the Pennsylvania Assembly sent Franklin to London to protest the actions of the colonial proprietors, the Penn family. Although he was not successful in that endeavor, he became known as the leading spokesman for America interests in England, living in that country for several extended periods.

"Writing the Declaration of Independence," by Jean Leon Gerome Ferris. From left to right: Benjamin Franklin, John Adams, and Thomas Jefferson.

By the time of his second return in 1775, the American Revolution had begun, and Franklin was unanimously chosen as Pennsylvania's delegate to the Second Continental Congress, where he became part of the Committee of Five that drafted the Declaration of Independence. During the war, Franklin served as Ambassador to France, and afterwards he was part of the convention that wrote the United States Constitution. He is the only founding father who signed all four of the key documents of the new nation: the Declaration of Independence, the Treaty of Alliance with France, the Treaty of Paris that ended the Revolutionary War, and the US Constitution.

Benjamin Franklin established a common law marriage with Deborah Read in 1730, and at the same time publicly acknowledged his son William, born out of wedlock. Later, father and son became estranged over American independence; William was an avid loyalist. The couple had two other children, one who died of smallpox at the age of four; the second, Sarah, cared for Benjamin in his old age.

Any short introduction to the life of Benjamin Franklin can only brush the surface of his life. He remains one of America's most beloved and respected figures.

January 17 Holidays and Celebrations

Kid Inventors' Day (United States)

Because Benjamin Franklin invented the first swim flippers at the age of 12, Kid Inventors' Day, celebrating past and present accomplishments of young inventors, is held each year on Franklin's birthday, January 17.

National Day (Minorca)

The Spanish island of Minorca, one of the Balearic Islands in the Mediterranean Sea, celebrates its National Day each year on January 17.

Patras Carnival (Greece)

The annual Patras Carnival, the largest event of its kind on Greece, begins each year on St. Anthony's Day, January 17, although its roots extend back to pagan times.

National Hot Buttered Rum Day (United States)

In the United States, almost every day of the year is dedicated to a particular food. Sponsored by manufacturers, retailers, farmers, or simply fans, these days are often proclaimed by the President, Congress, state governors, or mayors. Given that there are more different foods than days of the year, some days honor more than one kind of food!

January 17 is National Hot Buttered Rum Day. Hot Buttered Rum, a drink made of rum, butter, hot water or cider, and various spices, has its origin in colonial days and is particularly enjoyed in the winter months.

Christian Feast Days

In *Western Christianity*, Anthony the Great, Saint Jenaro Sánchez Delgadillo, Midgyth, and Sulptius the Pious are commemorated on January 17.

In *Eastern Orthodox Christianity*, it is the commemoration of Anthony the Great, Saint Theodosius the Great, Saint Ninnidh, four other saints named Anthony, and Saint Macarius. (These are observed on January 30 by "Old Calendarists.")

Other Holidays

Some holidays are simply made up by individuals, companies, or other organizations, and whether they become widely adopted depends on whether people choose to celebrate them. Here are some opportunities to celebrate on January 17.

January 17 is:

- Cable Car Day
- Ditch New Years Resolutions Day
- Hot Heads Chili Days
- Judgment Day
- Popeye Day

USAF F-14A Tomcat flying during Operation Desert Storm, which
began January 17, 1991

What Happened on January 17?

395 – The Roman Empire is Divided

On January 17, 395, the Roman emperor Theodosius the Great, died. In accordance with his will, his sons Arcadius and Honorius divided the empire. Honorius, who was only ten years old, was given the rulership of the west, and Arcadius, age 14, ruled the east. Both emperors were under the thumbs of their leading ministers.

Under Honorius, Rome was sacked for the first time in 800 years (the actual capital of the western Roman Empire, however, was in Milan). While the reign of Arcadius was less dramatic, he also accomplished little. Both emperors died in their thirties.

While the two halves of the empire had been growing apart since the reign of Constantine, this marked the final split. Although citizens of both east and west considered themselves part of the Roman Empire, historians mark this occasion as the end of a united Roman Empire and the beginning of the Byzantine Empire.

395 – The Papacy Returns to Rome

Because of a conflict between the French king Philip IV and the Pope, beginning in 1305, the seat of the papacy was moved from Rome to Avignon, where it remained through seven popes. In September 1376, Pope Gregory XI left Avignon and on January 17, 1377, reëstablished the Papal court in Rome. This did not resolve the conflict, for after Gregory's death, a schism in the church resulted in a second line of Avignon Popes, known as "antipopes." The conflict was not resolved until 1417, when the Catholic Church returned to having only a single pope.

1648 – The Vote of No Addresses

On January 17, 1648, a long-running conflict between the British monarch Charles I and Parliament came to a head when the "Long Parliament" voted to break off negotiations with the king in a document known as the "Vote of No Addresses." Fighting broke out between supporters of the king and supporters of Parliament, until the king's forces were defeated. Charles I was tried and executed, his son exiled, and the British monarchy overthrown. A republican Commonwealth of England, Ireland and Scotland, ruled over by Lord Protector Oliver Cromwell, took over until the restoration of the monarchy in 1660.

1781 – The Battle of Cowpens

Following several defeats of the Continental Army, a force of 800-, revolutionary soldiers commanded by General Daniel Morgan faced a elite British army of 1,150 commanded by General Banastre Tarleton. The battle was a decisive victory for the American side, with the British force suffering an 86 percent casualty rate. The psychological benefits to the revolutionary forces was substantial, and the Battle of Cowpens is considered a turning point in the American Revolutionary War.

Colonel William Washington at the Battle of Cowpens
(Art: S. H. Gimber)

1893 – Overthrow of the Kingdom of Hawaii

On January 17, 1893, a group of American and European business interests, calling themselves the "Committee of Safety," launched a coup d'état,

supported by a force of US Marines, to force the
Hawaiian Queen Lili'uokalani to abdicate the throne.
A provisional government gave rise to the Republic
of Hawaii, which lasted until the Hawaiian Islands
were annexed by the United States in 1898. Hawaii
became the 50th US state in 1959.

During the overthrow of the Hawaiian monarchy, the Household
Guard of Queen Liliuokalani is disarmed by members of the
"Committee of Safety."

1929 – Popeye Premiers

On January 17, 1929, a daily comic strip called
Thimble Theatre introduced a new character, Popeye
the Sailor Man. Although the ten-year old Thimble
Theatre had numerous characters, Popeye quickly
became its leading man. Beginning in 1933, Popeye
was featured in a series of popular cartoons by Max
Fleischer, and has since become a popular icon.

A World War II poster featuring Popeye the Sailor Man warns people about sharing potentially dangerous information.

1944 – The Battle of Monte Cassino

On January 17, 1944, Allied forces launched what would be the first of four assaults against the Axis "Winter Line" in an attempt to break through and capture Rome. Axis forces successfully defended their positions, and the three attacking divisions suffered nearly 4,000 casualties. Although the Allied forces ultimately succeeded, they suffered nearly 55,000 casualties, with the Axis suffering some 20,000 of its own.

A Sherman tank in the ruins of Monte Cassino

1945 – Raoul Wallenberg Arrested

Swedish diplomat and humanitarian Raoul Wallenberg, who had saved tens of thousands of Jews in Nazi-occupied Hungary, was detained in Budapest by the Soviets on January 17, 1945, on suspicion of espionage, and was never seen in public again. The exact reasons for Wallenberg's arrest and imprisonment, along with his ultimate fate, remain unknown, though reports claim he died in July 1947 in the Lubyanka, the KGB headquarters and secret prison in Moscow. His courage and humanitarianism have been widely celebrated and he has received numerous honors. The Raoul Wallenberg Award is given each year to persons who exemplify the "humanitarian ideals and the nonviolent courage" of Wallenberg.

Raoul Wallenberg

1946 – First Session of the UN Security Council

The Security Council of the United Nations is the only UN body with the authority to issue binding resolutions to member states. It has fifteen members, five of which are permanent. The permanent members of the Security Council, each of which has a veto, are the United States, the United Kingdom, Russia, France, and China. The other members are elected for two-year terms and do not have a veto power.

1950 – The Great Brink's Robbery

In what was then the largest robbery in the history of the United States, an eleven-member gang invaded the Brink's Building in Boston, Massachusetts on January 17, 1950, gagged and tied the employees, and stole $2,775 million (equivalent to $27.3 million in 2015). All eleven men were eventually arrested, and all but one (who died in prison) were paroled by 1971. Only $58,000 was ever recovered. At least four movies have been made about the robbery, most recently 1978's *The Brink's Job*.

1961 – Eisenhower Warns About the "Military-Industrial Complex"

In his farewell address as President of the United States on January 17, 1961, Dwight D. Eisenhower warned the nation, "[W]e must guard against the acquisition of unwarranted influence, whether sought or unsought, by the military–industrial complex."

1966 – The Palomares Incident

On January 17, 1966, a USAF B-52 bomber carrying four hydrogen bombs collided with a KC-135 tanker during a mid-air refueling over the Mediterranean Sea. All four of the tanker crew and three of the seven bomber crew died. Three of the nuclear weapons crashed near the Spanish village of Palomares. The non-nuclear triggering explosives in two of the weapons detonated on impact, contaminating a little less than a square mile (two square kilometers) with plutonium; the third landed in a riverbed and was relatively undamaged. The fourth bomb fell into the Mediterranean Sea, and was recovered intact after a two and a half month long search.

1991 – Operation Desert Storm Begins

Following the invasion and annexation of Kuwait by Iraq in August 1990, an international coalition led by the United States began Desert Shield, a buildup of troops and equipment to retake Kuwait. On January 17, 1991, the actual combat phase, named Desert Storm," began with a massive aerial bombardment campaign to destroy Iraq's Air Force and anti-aircraft facilities. By late February, armored forces of the US VII Corps had crossed into Iraq, supported by the XVIII Airborne Corps, with France's 6th Light Armored protecting the left flank, and by early March, active combat had ended with a decisive Coalition victory.

1998 – The Lewinsky Scandal Breaks

The website Drudge Report first reported the affair between US President Bill Clinton and White House intern Monica Lewinsky on January 17, 1998, and the report was quickly picked up by other media. This scandal led to the impeachment of Clinton by the House of Representatives, but after a 21-day trial in the US Senate, the President was acquitted of the charges of perjury and obstruction of justice.

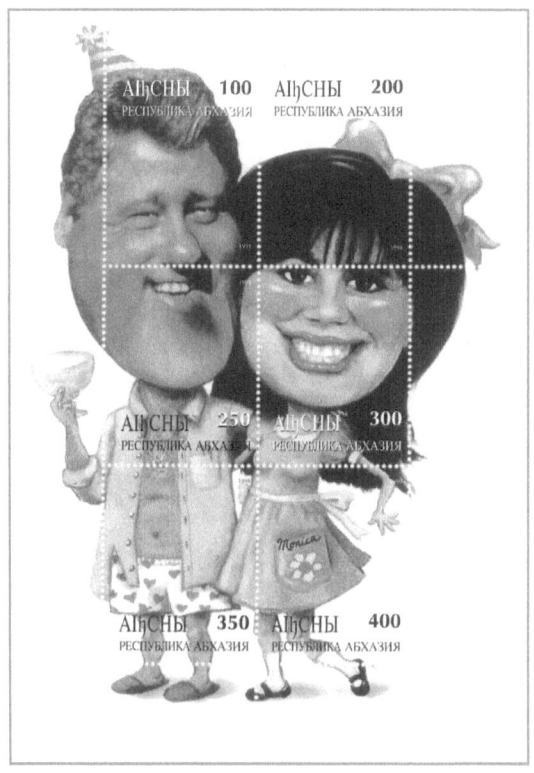

1998 postage stamps from the Abkhaz Republic lampooning the Lewinsky scandal

Who Was Born on January 17?

Art

Antonio Prohías (January 17, 1921 — February 24, 1998)

Cuban cartoonist Antonio Prohías created the long-running comic *Spy vs. Spy* for *Mad* magazine.

Logo from *Spy vs. Spy*

Business and Technology

Glenn L. Martin (January 17, 1886 — December 5, 1955)

Aviation pioneer Glenn L. Martin designed and built his own aircraft, and set aviation records. After several mergers, Martin's company is part of Lockheed Martin.

Crime

Edgar Ray Killen (January 17, 1925 —)

Ku Klux Klan leader Edgar Ray Killen planned and directed the 1964 "Mississippi Burning" murders of civil rights activists James Chaney, Andrew Goodman, and Michael Schwermer. He was not convicted until over 40 years after the crime, and received 60 years in prison for manslaughter.

Al Capone (January 17, 1899 — January 25, 1947)

Boss of the Chicago Outfit, gangster Al Capone became famous during the Prohibition era, making donations to charities to develop an image as a "modern-day Robin Hood" while running an increasingly violent bootlegging operation. He was responsible for the St. Valentine's Day Massacre. A special FBI team that became known as "the Untouchables" finally found evidence to have him convicted for tax evasion.

Arnold Rothstein (January 17, 1882 — November 6, 1928)

Kingpin of the New York Jewish mob in the early years of the 20th century, Arnold "the Brain" Rothstein is credited with turning organized crime into a big business. He leveraged Prohibition as a business opportunity, and was thought to have been responsible for fixing the 1919 World Series, known as the "Black Sox Scandal."

Al Capone

Fashion

Vidal Sassoon (January 17, 1928 — May 9, 2012)

Hairdresser and businessman Vidal Sassoon opened the first international chain of hairstyling salons and developed a line of hair products bearing his name. He invented the hairstyle known as the "wedge bob."

Government and Military

Michelle Obama (January 17, 1964 —)

Lawyer and writer Michelle Obama became the 44th First Lady of the United States upon the election of her husband Barack Obama, as well as the first African-American to hold that honor.

Michelle Obama (right) dancing with President Barack Obama
(Photo: D. B. King)

Robert F. Kennedy, Jr. (January 17, 1954 —)

Son of US Senator and Attorney-General Robert F. Kennedy and nephew of US President John F. Kennedy, Robert Kennedy Jr. is known as a radio host and environmental lawyer.

Douglas Wilder (January 17, 1931 —)

Upon his election as governor of Virginia, Douglas Wilder became the first African-American governor of any US state since Reconstruction. As lieutenant governor, he was the first African-American elected to statewide office in Virginia.

Newton N. Minow (January 17, 1926 —)

Former chair of the Federal Communications Commission Newton Minow is best known for his 1961 speech "Television and the Public Interest," in which he famously referred to commercial television programming as a "vast wasteland."

Nicholas Katzenbach (January 17, 1922 — May 8, 2012)

US Attorney General Nicholas Katzenbach confronted Alabama Governor George Wallace in the "Stand in the Schoolhouse Door" incident, in which Wallace attempted to deny black students admission to the University of Alabama.

John McCain, Jr. (January 17, 1911 — March 22, 1981)

US Navy Admiral John McCain, Jr., served as Commander-in-Chief, Pacific Command (CINCPAC), in charge of all US forces in the Vietnam thater from 1968 to 1972. His father, John McCain, Sr., was also an admiral during World War II, and the two are the first father and son pair to ever achieve four-star rank. His son, John McCain III, a naval aviator, was a POW in North Vietnam while his father was CINCPAC. McCain III subsequently became a US Senator and the 2008 Republican nominee for President.

David Lloyd George (January 17, 1863 — March 26, 1945)

David Lloyd George served as prime minister of the United Kingdom during World War I. He was voted the third-greatest British prime minister of the 20th century by historians, and one of the 100 greatest Britons in a UK-wide vote.

Douglas Hyde (January 17, 1860 — July 12, 1949)

Irish scholar Douglas Hyde served as the first President of Ireland, and played a major role in the Gaelic revival in that country.

Letters

Sebastian Junger (January 17, 1962 —)

Journalist Sebastian Junger is best known for his 1997 book *The Perfect Storm*, and for his documentary films about the war in Afghanistan, *Restrepo* and *Korengal.*

Nevil Shute (January 17, 1899 — January 12, 1960)

Aeronautical engineer Nevil Shute Norway used the pen name Nevil Shute for his best-selling novels, including the post-nuclear war novel *On the Beach*, which has been adapted twice as a film.

May Gibbs (January 17, 1877 — November 27, 1969)

Australian children's author May Gibbs wrote about "bush fairies." Her most famous work is called *Snugglepot and Cuddlepie.*

Anne Brontë (January 17, 1820 — May 28, 1849)

Youngest member of the Brontë literary family, Anne Brontë wrote *The Tenant of Wildfell Hall*, considered one of the first feminist novels. She died of tuberculosis at the age of 29.

Music

Kid Rock (January 17, 1971 —)

Singer-songwriter and rapper Kid Rock (Robert Ritchie) has sold over 25 million albums in the US and received five Grammy nominations.

Susanna Hoffs (January 17, 1959 —)

Susanna Hoffs is best known as a member of The Bangles.

Mick Taylor (January 17, 1949 —)

Guitarist and singer Mick Taylor was a member of The Rolling Stones from 1969 to 1974, and had previously been a member of John Mayall's Bluesbreakers. He was named one of the 100 greatest guitarists of all time by *Rolling Stone* magazine in 2011.

Mick Taylor (Photo: Dina Regine)

Dalida (January 17, 1933 — May 3, 1987)

Egyptian-born Italian singer and actress Iolanda Cristina Gigliotti, known by her stage name Dalida, is one of the six most popular singers in history, having sold over 170 million albums, including 80 gold records and the first-ever diamond record.

Eartha Kitt (January 17, 1927 — December 25, 2008)

Singer Eartha Kitt is best known for her 1953 recordings of "C'est Si Bon" and "Santa Baby." She also played Catwoman in the third season of the 1960's TV series *Batman*.

Eartha Kitt as Catwoman

Physical and Social Sciences

George Stigler (January 17, 1911 — December 1, 1991)

Economist George Stigler received the Nobel Prize in Economics in 1982 and the National Medal of Science in 1987 for his breakthrough contributions to the field.

August Weismann (January 17, 1834 — November 5, 1914)

Biologist August Weismann, described as "one of the great biologists of all time," developed the germ plasm theory, one of the underpinnings of modern evolutionary theory.

Leonard Fuchs (January 17, 1501 — May 10, 1566)

German physician and botanist Leonard Fuchs wrote and illustrated a large book about plants used in medicine. In honor of his achievement, the flower family Fuchsia (and the color fuchsia) are named for him. "Fuchsia" is often misspelled "fuschia," but it's easy to remember the right way: It's "Fuchs" + "ia"!

A fuchsia, named for Leonard Fuchs (Photo: Dirk van der Made)

Sports

Ann Wolfe (January 17, 1971 —)

Boxer Ann Wolfe held world titles in four different weight classes simultaneously, and is regarded as the best fighter in the history of women's boxing.

Maia Chiburdanidze (January 17, 1961 —)

Maia Chiburdanidze (მაია ჩიბურდანიძე) is the only chess player in history to have won nine Chess Olympiads, and the second woman to be awarded the title of grandmaster. She was Women's World Chess Champion from 1978 to 1991.

Muhammad Ali (January 17, 1942 —)

Boxer Muhammad Ali, born Cassius Clay, Jr., is widely considered one of the greatest heavyweights in the history of boxing and was named "Sportsman of the Century" by *Sports Illustrated*. He won the world heavyweight title three times, in 1964, 1974, and 1978, as well as an Olympic Gold Medal in boxing in 1960.

Muhammad Ali (Photo: Ira Rosenberg)

Don Zimmer (January 17, 1931 — June 4, 2014)

Don Zimmer was involved in professional baseball as an infielder, manager, and coach for 65 years. He received a brain injury from being hit by a pitch, resulting in the adoption of batting helmets as a safety measure.

Jacques Plante (January 17, 1929 — February 27, 1986)

Considered one of the most important innovators in hockey, Jacques Plante was inducted into the Hockey Hall of Fame in 1978.

Corsica Joe (January 17, 1920 — March 14, 2010)

Professional wrestler Francois Miquet, known by his ring name of "Corsica Joe," was named to the NWA Hall of Fame in 2008.

Cus D'Amato (January 17, 1908 — November 4, 1985)

Boxing manager and trainer Cus D'Amato handled the careers of three members of the International Boxing Hall of Fame: Mike Tyson, Floyd Patterson, and José Torres.

Busher Jackson (January 17, 1911 — June 25, 1966)

Busher Jackson was named to five NHL All-Star teams and was inducted into the Hockey Hall of Fame in 1971 after his nomination had been repeatedly blocked because of personal problems, including alcoholism.

Theater, Television, and Film

Zooey Deschanel (January 17, 1980 —)

Zooey Deschanel has appeared in numerous movies. She is best known for her role on the sitcom *New Girl*.

Jim Carrey (January 17, 1962 —)

Actor and comedian Jim Carrey is known for his roles in such films as *Ace Ventura: Pet Detective, Dumb and Dumber, The Mask, The Truman Show,* and *Man on the Moon,* in which he played Andy Kaufman (born January 17, 1949).

Jim Carrey (Photo: Jean-François Gornet)

Steve Harvey (January 17, 1957 —)

Radio and television personality Steve Harvey is known for hosting talk shows bearing his name as well as hosting the game show *Family Feud*.

Andy Kaufman (January 17, 1949 — May 16, 1984)

Performance artist Andy Kaufman was known for his role as Latka Gravis on the TV series *Taxi,* as well as for his stand-up comedy.

Maury Povich (January 17, 1939 —)

Maury Povich is best known as the host of the eponymous tabloid talk show *Maury.*

Shari Lewis (January 17, 1933 — August 2, 1998)

Ventriloquist and puppeteer Shari Lewis is known for her puppet creation Lamb Chop, and hosted several children's programs in her long career. She wrote over 60 books for children, as well an episode of the original *Star Trek* television series.

Shari Lewis with Lamb Chop (left) and Charlie Horse (right)

James Earl Jones (January 17, 1931 —)

In his distinguished acting career, James Earl Jones
has received a Tony Award, a Golden Globe, three
Emmys, and an Academy Award nomination. His
best known roles include playing Jack Jefferson in
The Great White Hope. the voice of Darth Vader in the
Star Wars films, and Mufasa in Disney's *The Lion
King*.

James Earl Jones in a 2013 stage production of
Driving Miss Daisy (Photo: Eva Rinaldi)

Moira Shearer (January 17, 1926 — January 31, 2005)

Ballet dancer and actress Moira Shearer is best known for her role in the 1948 film *The Red Shoes*.

Betty White (January 17, 1922 —)

Actress and comedienne Betty White is known for her roles on the sitcoms *The Mary Tyler Moore Show* and *The Golden Girls,* and most recently on *Hot in Cleveland.*

Betty White (r) with husband and game show host Allen Ludden

Mack Sennett (January 17, 1880 — November 5, 1960)

Silent film director Mack Sennett (left) is known for his slapstick comedies, most famously the Keystone Cops films, which he produced.

Konstantin Stanislavsky (January 17 [O.S. January 5], 1863 — August 7, 1938)

Actor and theater director Konstantin Stanislavsky (Константи́н Станисла́вский) is best known for the "Stanislavsky method" for actors (often referred to as "method acting"), and had a major impact on both the Russian and American stage. His teachings are widely used to this day.

Who Died on January 17?

Art

Louis Comfort Tiffany (February 18, 1848 — January 17, 1933)

Artist and designer Louis Comfort Tiffany is known for his work in stained glass, and also served as design director for the jewelry company Tiffany & Co., founded by his father.

Tiffany stained glass window from the New York Historical Society (Photo: Griannan)

Crime

Yevgeny Ivanov (January 11, 1926 — January 17, 1994)

Soviet spy Yevgeny Ivanov, posing as a naval attaché, triggered the British scandal known as the Profumo affair when it was revealed that his mistress Christine Keeler was also lovers with Britain's defense minister, John Profumo.

Gary Gilmore (December 4, 1940 — January 17, 1977)

Convicted murderer Gary Gilmore gained notoriety for demanding that his death sentence be carried out, and became the first person in the US to be executed in nearly ten years.

Government and Public Affairs

James Hood (November 10, 1942 — January 17, 2013)

James Hood was one of the first African-Americans to enroll at the University of Alabama, and became famous when Alabama Governor George Wallace blocked him from enrolling in what became known as the "Stand in the Schoolhouse Door."

Barbara Jordan (February 21, 1936 — January 17, 1996)

Civil rights leader Barbara Jordan was the first African-American elected to the Texas Senate since Reconstruction and the first southern black female elected to the House of Representatives. Among her many honors is the Presidential Medal of Freedom.

Juliette Gordon Low (October 31, 1860 — January 17, 1927)

Juliette Gordon Low founded the Girl Scouts of the USA, serving as the organization's first president.

Rutherford B. Hayes (October 11, 1822 — January 17, 18933)

18th President of the United States, Rutherford B. Hayes lost the popular vote but won a hotly disputed battle in the Electoral College in exchange for the Compromise of 1877, ending Reconstruction in the post-Civil War South.

Rutherford B. Hayes

Theodosius the Great (January 11, 347 — January 17, 395)

Roman emperor Theodosius I was the last emperor to rule over both the eastern and western halves of the empire. He also made Nicene Christianity the official state religion of the empire. For the aftermath of his death, see "What Happened on January 17."

Theodosius I the Great

Letters

Erich Segal (June 16, 1937 — January 17, 2010)

Erich Segal is best known for his 1970 novel *Love Story*, and also wrote the screenplay for the film version.

Art Buchwald (October 20, 1925 — January 17, 2007)

Journalist and humorist Art Buchwald is known for his long-running syndicated column, for which he received the Pulitzer Prize in 1982.

Betty Smith (December 15, 1896 — January 17, 1972)

Betty Smith is best known for her first novel, *A Tree Grows in Brooklyn*.

T. H. White (May 29, 1906 — January 17, 1964)

Author T. H. White is best known for his Arthurian novel series *The Once and Future King*. The first section, *The Sword in the Stone*, was made into a Walt Disney film in 1963.

Music

Johnny Otis (December 28, 1921 — January 17, 2012)

Known as the original "King of Rock and Roll" and the "Godfather of Rhythm and Blues," impressario Johnny Otis co-wrote "Hound Dog," "Every Beat of My Heart," and "Willie and the Hand Jive." He has been inducted into both the Rock and Roll Hall of Fame and the Blues Hall of Fame.

Don Kirshner (April 17, 1934 — January 17, 2011)

Music publisher, producer, and songwriter Don Kirshner was known as "The Man with the Golden Ear." He managed such pop groups as The Monkees, The Archies, and Kansas, and helped launch the careers of Bobby Darin, Neil Diamond, and Carole King.

Science and Medicine

Clyde Tombaugh (February 16, 1822 — January 17, 1911)

Astronomer Clyde Tombaugh discovered the dwarf planet Pluto in 1930.

Francis Galton (February 16, 1822 — January 17, 1911)

Polymath Sir Francis Galton published over 340 papers and books in his distinguished career. Among his many accomplishments, he created the statistical concept of correlation and regression toward the man, coined the expression "nature versus nurture," founded the science of psychometrics and differential psychology, developed a method for classifying fingerprints, and devised the first weather map.

Chang and Eng Bunker (May 11, 1811 — January 17, 1874)

Conjoined twins Chang and Eng Bunker, originally from Thailand, were exhibited worldwide as a curiosity, and gave rise to the term "Siamese Twins." Later in life, they purchased a farm in North Carolina, married sisters, and gave birth to a combined 21 children.

Chang and Eng Bunker

Sports

Bobby Fischer (March 9, 1943 — January 17, 2008)

Bobby Fischer was given the title of chess grandmaster at the age of 15, and at 20 won the US Championship with the only perfect score in the history of the tournament. He became world chess champion in 1972, defeating Boris Spassky in the most famous chess championship ever played.

Bobby Fischer

Theater, Television, and Film

Virginia Mayo (November 30, 1920 — January 17, 2005)

Best known for her comedy films with Danny Kaye, including *The Secret Life of Walter Mitty*, Mayo also played gold-digger Marie Derry in the 1946 film *The Best Years of Our Lives*.

Virginia Mayo (right) with Gene Nelson in 1952's *She's Working Her Way Through College*

Richard Crenna (November 30, 1926 — January 17, 2003)

Actor Richard Crenna starred in numerous movies, as well as in the sitcom *The Real McCoys*.

Doodles Weaver (May 11, 1911 — January 17, 1983)

Comedian, actor and musician Doodles Weaver performed on Rudy Vallée's radio program, hosted his own variety show, was a member of Spike Jones' City Slickers, and was an early contributor to *Mad* magazine. He appeared in more than 90 films and numerous TV series.

Evelyn Nesbit (December 25, 1884 — January 17, 1967)

Evelyn Nesbit was one of the most famous faces of her age, immortalized by architect Stanford White as "The Girl in the Red Velvet Swing." Her jealous husband, Harry Kendall Thaw, shot and killed White, leading to what was then referred to as the "Trial of the Century."

Evelyn Nesbit

Lola Montez (February 17, 1821 — January 17, 1861)

Actress and dancer Lola Montez became the mistress of King Ludwig I of Bavaria, using her influence to institute liberal reforms. She was forced to flee following the revolutions of 1848, and spent the remainder of her life in the United States.

Lola Montez (Portrait by Joseph Karl Stieler)

Michael Dobson

January, by Hans Thoma

January:
The First Month

That blasts of January
Would blow you through and through.

— William Shakespeare, The Winter's Tale

January wasn't always the first month in the year. In ancient Rome, March was the first month until about 450 BCE. Even after January became the official first month in the calendar, Romans still counted dates from the inauguration of the consuls, March 15 and May 1.

In the Middle Ages, Christian feast days were used to start the new year, including March 25 and December 25. It wasn't until the 16th century that European nations made January 1 the official start of the new year. (This was called "Circumcision Style" because January 1 was also celebrated as the Feast of the Circumcision of Jesus.)

The name January (*Ianuarius*) is derived from the Roman god Janus, the god of beginning and transitions. Janus gives his name to the Latin word for door (*ianua*), because January is the door to the year. Janus is normally portrayed as having two faces, one looking toward the future and one toward the past. In spite of that, the goddess Juno was the patron of that month.

In both the Julian and Gregorian calendars (see "What Day of the Week..."), January is the first month of the year and one of seven months with 31 days. In the Northern Hemisphere, January is the coldest month of the year, and in the Southern Hemisphere, it's the warmest, equivalent to the Northern Hemisphere's July.

January in Other Cultures

The month of January has different names in different languages. Some nations use calendars other than the Gregorian, and their months may overlap with January. In lunar-based calendars, such as the Islamic calendar, months move through the seasons. Still, many languages often have a word for January itself.

Albanian: Janar

Anglo-Saxon: Wulf-monath

Arabic (Egypt, Sudan, Yemen): يونَأغيناير (*yanāyir*)

Arabic (Levant): حزيركانون الثاني (*kānūn al-thānī*)

Arabic (Libya): الصهنار (*aynu n-nār*)

Arabic (Algeria and Tunisia): جأينجانفي (*Jānfī*)

Arabic (Morocco): غيناير (*yanāyər*)

Azerbaijani: Yanvar

Basque: Urtarril

Bulgarian: януари (*januari*)

Chinese: 一月 (Cantonese: *yātyuht*; Mandarin: *yīyuè*; Taiwanese: *it-goeh*)

Corsican: Ghjennaghju

Croatian: Siječanj

Czech: Leden

Finnish: Tammikuu (oak moon)

French: Janvier

German/Danish/Norwegian/Slovenian: Januar

Greek: Ιανουάριος (*Ianouários*)

Haitian Creole: Janvye

Hebrew: ינואר (*yanû'ar*)

Hindi: जनवरी (*janvarī*)

Hungarian: Január

Irish (Gaelic): Eanáir mí Eanáir

Italian: Gennaio

Japanese: 一月 (*ichigatsu*), 睦月 (*mutsuki*)

Kazakh: Қаңтар (*Ķaņtar*)

Korean: 일월 (*ilweol*)

Lithuanian: Sausis

Maori: Kohitātea

Old English: Se æfterra Gēola

Polish: Styczeń

Portuguese: Janeiro

Russian: январь (*janvar'*)

Scottish Gaelic: am Faoilleach

Sesotho: Pherekgong

Slovene: Prosinec

Spanish: Enero

Swahili/Dutch/Swedish: Januari

Swazi: Bhimbidvwane

Thai: มกราคม (*makarakhom*)

Turkish: Ocak

Vietnamese: 腑乂 (*tháng một*)

Walloon: Djanvî

Welsh: Ionawr

Yiddish: אויגויאַנואַר (*yanuar*)

Zulu: uJanuwari

January Sayings and Superstitions

Here are some sayings and superstitions associated with the month of January.

New Year Superstitions

It's important to kiss those dearest to us at the stroke of the New Year to keep their affections for the next twelve months.

The new year must not be seen with bare cupboards. Stock up on supplies and make sure there's plenty of money in ever wallet in the home.

Do not begin the new year with the household in debt.

The first person to enter your home after the stroke of midnight will tell you the kind of year you will have.

Do not let anything leave your house on the first day of the year, not even garbage.

Start your year off with good luck by eating hoppin' john, a dish made with black-eyed peas and rice (southern United States).

Wear something new on January 1.

Be sure to open the door at midnight to let the old year escape.

Babies born on New Year's Day will always have good luck.

January Wedding Superstitions

A January bride will be a prudent housekeeper, and very good tempered.

Married in January's hoar and rime / Widowed you'll be before your prime.

Married when the year is new, he'll be loving, kind and true.

January Symbols

Birthstone: Garnet, representing constancy.

Soviet postage stamp showing a geologist finding garnets

Birth Flower (Britain): Carnation, representing love, fascination, and distinction

Vase with Red and White Carnation on a Yellow Background,
by Vincent van Gogh

Birth Flower (America): Carnation or Snowdrop (*Galanthus*)

A New Year's greeting card with snowdrops

Birth Flower (China): Plum blossom (*prunus mume*)

Red Plum Blossom (Photo: Frank Gualtieri)

Birth Flower (Japan): Camellia

Camellias (Clara Maria Pope)

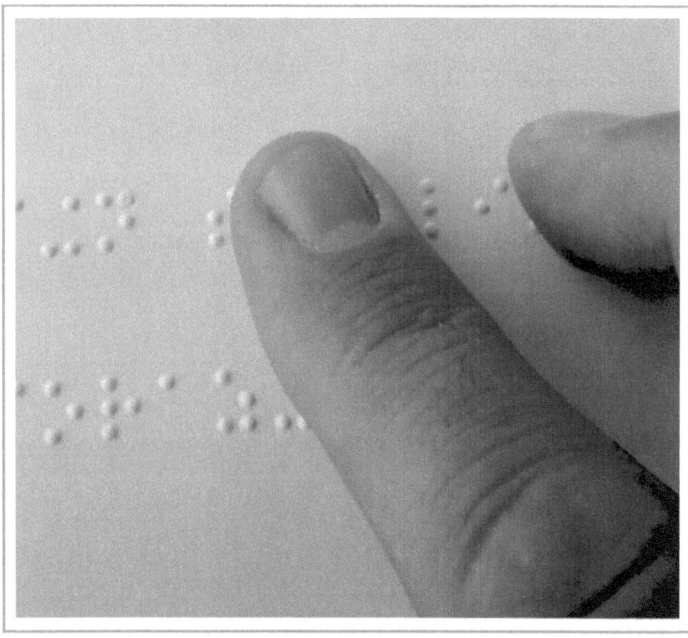

A person reading a braille book, for National Braille Literacy Month
(Photo: Antonio X Alonso)

January Events

Honorary Months

Presidents, Congresses, and nations around the world issue proclamations recognizing particular months to honor certain causes. These events generally fall in June, though honorary months do come and go. Holidays established by states and nonprofit organizations are listed if verified. If not otherwise specified, all months are US. There is some variation from year to year; some celebratory months get added and others get dropped. Two places to get up to date information are the current edition of *Chase's Calendar of Events* or the website www.brownielocks.com/january.html.

- Adopt a Rescued Bird Month
- Bath Safety Month
- Be Kind to Food Servers Month
- Birth Defects Month
- California Dried Plum Digestive Month
- Cervical Health Awareness Month
- Financial Wellness Month
- Get Organized Month
- International Child-Centered Divorce Awareness Month
- International Creativity Month
- **National Braille Literacy Month**
- National Clean Up Your Computer Month
- National Codependency Awareness Month
- National Mentoring Month

- National Polka Music Month
- National Poverty in America Awareness Month
- National Skating Month
- National Soup Month
- National Thank You Month
- National Volunteer Blood Donor Month
- Oatmeal Month
- Slavery and Human Trafficking Prevention Month
- Stalking Awareness Month
- Teen Driving Awareness Month
- Train Your Dog Month (also Walk Your Dog Month)
- Weight Loss Awareness Month

Moveable and Multi-Day Events

Some events take place over a specific week or time period. Start and finish dates may vary from year to year. Some events occur on different days each year (such as "fourth Saturday of a month"). These events sometimes take place on this day.

3rd Sunday (January 15-21)

- Pongal (India)
- Feast of the *Santo Niño* (Philippines)

Martin Luther King, Jr., Day

Civil rights leader Martin Luther King, Jr., was born January 15, 1929. The US holiday in his honor is celebrated on the third Monday in January, so in different years can fall anywhere from January 15 through 21.

Martin Luther King, Jr. (Photo: Dick DeMarsico, New York World-Telegram and the Sun Newspaper)

Non-Gregorian Events

Not every culture uses the familiar Gregorian calendar, so some events not only shift within a range of a few days depending on the year, but may even migrate through the months. Here is a selection of events around the world that sometimes take place on January 17.

- Dhanurmas (Hindu calendar)
- Thiruvathira (Hinduism, Tamil calendar)
- Lohri (Punjab)
- Thai Pongal (Hinduism, Tamil calendar)
- Mattu Pongal (Hinduism, Tamil calendar)
- Makara Sankranthi (Hinduism)
- Thaipusam (Hinduism, Tamil calendar)
- Tu B'Shevat

January Zodiac Signs

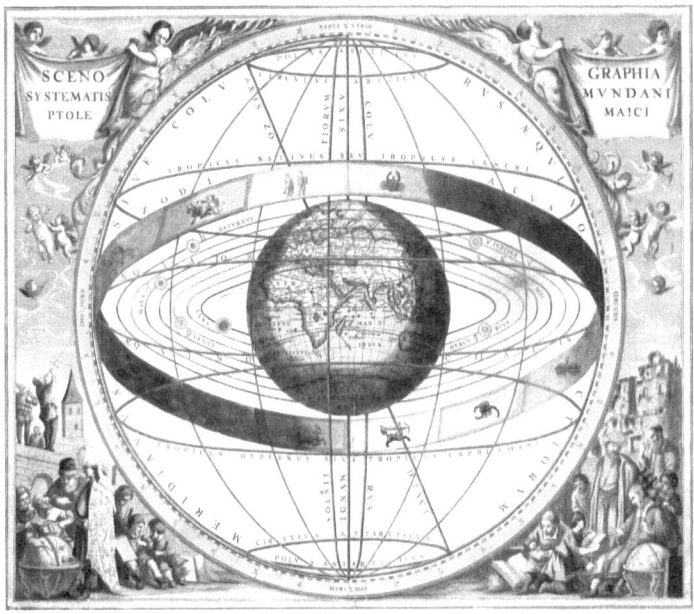

Scenography of the Ptolemaic Cosmography, by Johannes van Loon, based on Andreas Cellarius's *Harmonia Macrocosmica,* 1660

January Zodiac Signs

From the perspective of someone on Earth, the Sun appears to move through the sky throughout the year, along a path astronomers call the *ecliptic plane*. The ecliptic plane is divided into twelve constellations, known as the zodiac, based on traditionally observed patterns of stars. On your birthday, you can't see your constellation, because it's in the daytime sky.

The zodiac was first developed by Babylonian astronomers about 2,500 years ago. Because they were unaware that the Earth wobbles like a spinning top (known as *precession*), they didn't make allowance for the fact that the Sun's path through the zodiac changes over time.

That means there are now two sets of dates for your birth sign. The *tropical dates* are the original Babylonian dates; the *sidereal dates* tell you where the Sun actually appears as it moves along its annual path.

While most dates have different signs for the tropical and sidereal signs, January 17 is unusual that both are the same: Capricorn.

Capricorn

Tropical December 22 to January 20
Sidereal January 15 to February 14

The origins of the constellation Capricorn date back to Sumeria and Babylonia. Based on Enki, the Sumerian god of wisdom and waters, Capricorn has the head and upper body of a mountain goat and the lower body and tail of a fish. The mountain goat represents ambition and intelligence, the fish represents passion and spirituality.

An earth sign, Capricorn is ruled by the planet Saturn. They are often thought to be responsible, patient, ambitious and loyal, but can sometimes be seen as conceited, distrusting, and unimaginative. Capricornians are supposed to be compatible with Taurus, Pisces, and Virgo, but not with Aries, Sagittarius, or Leo.

Illustration by Edward Penfield

What Day of the Week is January 17?

On what day of the week does January 17 fall?

Surprisingly, this isn't an easy question. Because the calendar year is 365 days long (366 in leap years), it doesn't divide evenly by the seven days of the week.

Also, the Earth goes around the Sun in about 365-1/4 days, so a calendar tends to drift over time. That's why the same date falls on different weekdays in different years.

This is made even more complicated by a change in calendars that took place in 1582. Our modern calendar has its roots in ancient Rome, in a calendar reform conducted by Julius Caesar. Caesar commissioned mathematicians to attack the problem, and they came up with the idea of leap years, and thus standardized the calendar for centuries to come. This was called the Julian calendar.

Over time, however, the small errors in Caesar's calculation compounded. That's why Pope Gregory XIII commissioned the Gregorian calendar, used in most of the world today. Some countries converted in 1582, when the calendar was first developed; some converted later; other still haven't changed.

Gregorian and Julian aren't the only types of calendars. The Hebrew year, the Islamic year, and many other calendars are used in different parts of the world and among different people.

You can convert Gregorian dates to other calendars, including the Hebrew calendar, the Islamic calendar, and even the Mayan calendar by visiting the Fourmilab Calendar Converter at http://www.fourmilab.ch/documents/calendar/.

Chinese calendar systems are quite complex and have changed several times; a full discussion is far beyond the scope of this book. If you're interested, you can find information here: http://www.hermetic.ch/cal_stud/chinese_cal.htm.

On Names and Dates

Historians use "CE" (Common Era) and "BCE" (Before the Common Era) instead of the more common "AD" (Anno Domini, or Year of Our Lord) and "BC" (Before Christ), reflecting the fact that the year-numbering system established by the Gregorian calendar is used throughout the world in many countries not culturally Christian.

The CE/BCE designation dates back to at least 1708, and has been adopted as a standard by the United Nations and the Universal Postal Union. Because this series of books covers events and people of all nations and cultures, we use the CE/BCE style.

The abbreviation "O.S." ("Old Style") on some dates refers to the fact that not all nations switched from the Julian to the Gregorian calendar at the same time. (The first nations switched in 1582, the Russian

Empire did not do so until 1918.) Therefore some figures and events have two dates, with the Julian date given the "O.S." designation.

Also, in the Julian calendar in England in the 16th century, the year began on March 25 rather than January 1. To avoid confusion with Gregorian dates, dates between January and March were often (but not always) written using both years.

People and events whose original names are not in the Western alphabet have their native names (where possible) in the appropriate script shown in parenthesis. If you are using an e-reader to access an electronic version of this book, all characters don't always display on all devices.

A 50-year brass perpetual calendar.

Cartoon by John T. McCutcheon

Copyright, Credit, and Contact

Follow Us

Our blog Dobson's Improbable History (http://
improbhistory.blogspot.com) features short articles on events
and people associated with each day, and updates several
times each week. You can also get a daily "What Happened
In History" message and all the latest Timespinner Press
news by following us on Facebook at https://
www.facebook.com/TimespinnerPress. Our Twitter feed
@SidewiseThinker links you to all our News of the Day.

Contact Us

Find an error or a format problem? Want information about
the series, about us, or about when the volume for your
special day might be available? Please email us at
editor@timespinnerpress.com. (We also take requests if your
special day isn't yet complete. Please give us at least six
weeks' notice if possible.)

Sources

We owe a great debt to Wikipedia, which is our first stop for
research. We attempt to make independent confirmation of
all important dates and facts through a variety of other
sources. Other sources we frequently use include the Library
of Congress; "on this day" listings from *Encyclopedia
Britannica*, the *New York Times*, and the BBC; Omniglot for the

names of months in other languages; *Chase's Calendar of Events*; and, of course, the always essential Google.

All art and photographs are either in the public domain, used under a Creative Commons license, or with a "fair use" justification, and most frequently come from Wikimedia Commons and the Library of Congress Prints and Photographs Division.

Attribution is provided where possible, or as requested by the copyright owner, or when there is particular historical significance, listed below. For information about any particular illustration or photograph, please contact us.

Credits

- The cover painting, "Benjamin Franklin Drawing Electricity from the Sky," was created circa 1816 by Benjamin West, and is in the public domain because its copyright has expired. It is in the collection of the Philadelphia Museum of Art; the image is from Google Art Project by way of Wikimedia Commons.

- The illustration of the month of January used on the back cover is from the French Gothic illuminated manuscript *Les Très Riches Heures du duc de Berry* by the Limbourg Brothers, Jean Colombe, and an intermediate painter whose name is lost to history. It is in the public domain because its copyright has expired.

- "The Month of January" used as the frontispiece is from the *Grimani Breviary*, created sometime between 1490 and 1510. It is in the public domain because its copyright has expired. The illuminated manuscript is in the collection of the Biblioteca Marciana, Venice, Italy.

- The 1778 portrait of Benjamin Franklin by Joseph-Siffrein Duplessis is in the public domain because its copyright has expired. The original is in the collection of the National Portrait Gallery, London.

- The 1739 edition of *Poor Richard's Almanack* is from the Library of Congress Rare Book and Special Collections Division. The original is in the public domain because its copyright has expired; the image is in the public domain as a work created by an employee or officer of the U.S. government as part of that person's official duties.

- The painting "Writing the Declaration of Independence" by Jean Leon Gerome Ferris is in the public domain because its copyright has expired. The painting is in the collection of the Virginia Historical Society and is also available from the Library of Congress using digital ID cph.3g09904.

- The US Navy photograph of an F-14A Tomcat during Operation Desert Storm is in the public domain as a work created by an officer or employee of the US federal government.

- The engraving of Colonel William Washington at the Battle of Cowpens was created by S. H. Gimber for *Graham's Magazine*. It is in the collection of the US National Archives and Records Administration (ARC identifier 532886), and is in the public domain.

- The cartoon of Popeye the Sailor Man was created by the government of the United Kingdom during World War II, and is in the public domain.

- The photograph of the disarming of Queen Liliuokalani's Household Guard in 1893 is by J. J. Williams, and is in the collection of the Hawaii State Archives (Call Number PP-54-1-001). It is in the public domain because its copyright has expired.

- The photograph "A Sherman tank of 19th Armoured Regiment, 4th New Zealand Armoured Brigade supporting infantry of 6th NZ Infantry Brigade, during a reconstruction of the action at Cassino, Italy, 8 April 1944" is from the collection of the Imperial War Museum (NA 13800), and is in the public domain as a work created by the the the United Kingdom Government prior to 1957.

- The photograph of Raoul Wallenberg is in the public domain.

- The Abkhaz Republic postage stamps about the Lewinsky scandal are not an object of copyright according to the Law of the Abkhaz Republic 1227-c-XIV of January 16, 2006, Article 8.

- The comic strip *Spy vs. Spy* is a copyright and trademark of *Mad* magazine. The use here is under "fair use" rationale. It illustrates an article about the artist in question, its size and resolution is too low to permit the creation of counterfeit goods, and there is no free media equivalent available.

- The 1929 mug shot of Al Capone is in the public domain as a work created by an official of the US federal government as part of his or her official duties.

- The 2009 photograph of President Barack Obama and First Lady Michelle Obama dancing was taken by D. B. King and is used here under CC BY-SA 2.0.

- The 1972 or 1973 photograph of Mick Taylor was taken by Dina Regine and is used here under CC BY-SA 2.0.

- The 1967 publicity photograph of Eartha Kitt as Catwoman from the TV series *Batman* is in the public domain because it was first published in the United States between 1923 and 1977 without a copyright notice. Traditionally, publicity photographs are not copyrighted because of the way in which they are intended to be used.

- The photograph of a *fuchsia jimenezii* was taken by Dirk van der Made and is used here under CC BY-SA 3.0.

- The 1967 "work made for hire" photograph of Muhammad Ali by Ira Rosenberg is part of the New York *World-Telegram and Sun* collection donated to the Library of Congress. Per the instrument of gift it is in the public domain.

- The 1960 publicity photograph of Shari Lewis is in the public domain because it was first published in the United States between 1923 and 1977 without a copyright notice. Traditionally, publicity photographs are not copyrighted because of the way in which they are intended to be used.

- The 2010 photograph of Jim Carrey was taken by Jean-François Gornet and is used here under CC BY-SA 2.0.

- The 2010 photograph of James Earl Jones in a stage production of *Driving Miss Daisy* is by Eva Rinaldi and is used here under CC BY-SA 2.0.

- The 1963 publicity photograph of Allen Ludden and Betty White is in the public domain because it was first published in the United States between 1923 and 1977 without a copyright notice. Traditionally, publicity photographs are not copyrighted because of the way in which they are intended to be used.

- The 1919 promotional photograph of Mack Sennett is in the public domain because its copyright has expired.
- The photograph of a Tiffany landscape window was taken by "griannan" as part of the Wikipedia Loves Art project, and is used here under CC BY-SA 2.5.
- The 1877 portrait of Rutherford B. Hayes is in the public domain because its copyright has expired.
- The 1836 portrait of Theodosius I is in the public domain because its copyright has expired.
- The photograph of Chang and Eng Bunker is in the public domain because its copyright has expired.
- The 1960 photograph of Bobby Fischer is Bundesarchiv Bild 183-76052-0335, and is used here under CC BY-SA 3.0.
- The 1952 publicity photograph of Gene Nelson and Virginia Mayo in *She's Working Her Way Through College* is in the public domain because it was first published in the United States between 1923 and 1977 without a copyright notice. Traditionally, publicity photographs are not copyrighted because of the way in which they are intended to be used.
- The 1900 photograph of Evelyn Nesbit is from the Library of Congress Prints and Photographs Division (ppmsca.12056) and is in the public domain because its copyright has expired.
- The 1847 painting of Lola Montez by Joseph Karl Stieler was painted for King Ludwig I of Bavaria and is in the Gallery of Beauties, Nymphenburg Place, Munich. It is in the public domain because its copyright has expired.
- The painting *January* is from the calendar book *Festkalender* by Hans Thoma. It is in the pubic domain because its copyright has expired.
- The 1968 USSR postage stamp "Prospecting Geologist with Found Diamond and Red Crystals-Pyropes (Garnets)" is not an object of copyright according to Part IV of Civil Code No. 230-FZ of the Russian Federation (2006).
- The 1886 painting "Vase with Red and White Carnations on a Yellow Background" by Vincent Van Gogh is in the public domain because its copyright has expired.
- The German New Year's greeting card was made circa 1900. It is in the public domain because its copyright has expired.

- The 2006 photograph of a red plum blossom (*prunus mume*) was taken by Frank Gualtieri, who released the photograph into the public domain.

- The illustration of camellias by Clara Maria Pope is from Samuel Curtis' *Monograph on the Genus Camellia*, published in 1819. It is in the public domain because its copyright has expired.

- The photograph of a person reading a braille book was taken by Antonio X. Alonso in 2009. It is used here under CC BY-SA 2.0.

- The 1964 photograph of Dr. Martin Luther King, Jr., was taken by Dick DeMarisco for the *New York World Telegram and Sun*. It is part of a collection donated by the Word Telegram and Sun to the Library of Congress (digital ID cph. 3c22988), and per the instrument of gift, it is in the public domain.

- The celestial sphere is from *Scenography of the Ptolemaic Cosmography*, by Johannes van Loon, based on Andreas Cellarius's *Harmonia Macrocosmica*, 1660. It is in the public domain because its copyright has expired.

- The 1906 automobile calendar is by Edward Penfield, and is in the collection of the Library of Congress Prints and Photographs Division. It is in the public domain because its copyright has expired.

- The 50-year perpetual calendar photograph is in the public domain.

- The cartoon by John T. McCutcheon is from his 1905 collection *The Mysterious Stranger and Other Cartoons by John T. McCutcheon*. It is in the public domain because its copyright has expired.

License Description and Terms

Aside from material purely in the public domain, photographs and other material in this book are used under specific licenses permitting free use, usually with an attribution requirement. For full text and terms of these licenses, click or enter the appropriate links below. If you believe there is an error in the copyright status or attribution of any of these images, please email us.

Timespinner
Press

Other Books from Timespinner Press

The Story of a Special Day
Michael Dobson

A series of (eventually) 366 volumes covering everything that happened on your special day! Events, births, deaths, quotes, holidays, and much more. It's like a birthday card they'll never throw away! Don't see your date available yet? Just write us!

US$7.95 print / US$2.99 ebook.

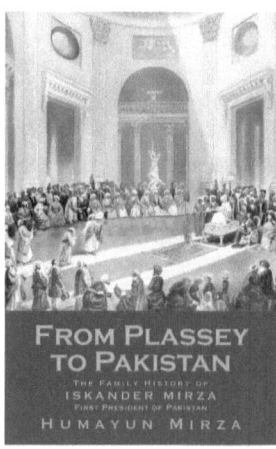

From Plassey to Pakistan
Humayun Mirza

The history of British Colonial India and the formation of Pakistan from the unique perspective of the son of Pakistan's first president and last of the royal line of Bengal, Bihar, and Orissa! This unique historical document tells the inside story of this distinguished family, including the detailed story of the coup that toppled his father from power!

US$27.95 print

A Whole New Navy: America's War in the Pacific

Miles Durr

The most comprehensive and detailed description of America's naval war in the Pacific ever—every battle, every ship, every task force and every task group from Pearl Harbor through the Japanese surrender! A must-have for the collection of every World War II buff!

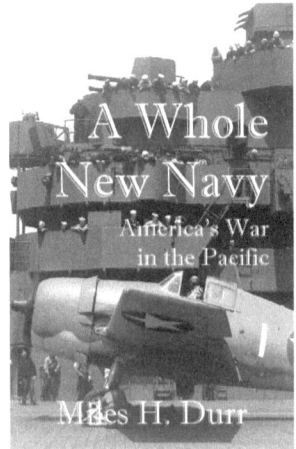

US$29.95 print

Improbable History: The Weird, the Obscure, and the Strangely Important

edited by Michael Dobson

From the birth of Western civilization to the rescue of Apollo 13, from the Leaning Tower of Pisa to Florence's Duomo, history has often turned on small, improbable details. Whatever happened to the ancient Samaritan people? Why did a fortuitous rainstorm allow the British to conquer India? How did an air raid in Italy lead to the development of chemotherapy? What happened when Albert Einstein met Adolf Hitler on the streets of Berlin? How did the Japanese manage to attack the US mainland using balloons? A cast of award-winning writers tackle some of the strangest tales in history!

US$19.95 print